IMPLEMENTING ITIL SERVICE MANAGEMENT, NOT AN 'OUT OF THE BOX' APPROACH

By: Ivanka Menken

CONTENTS

INTRODUCTION

Even after 13 years in IT Service Management consultancy, I still get questions from clients about the duration of ITIL®[i] implementation projects.

It seems that a lot of people 'out there' still seem to think that an ITIL implementation project is similar to the rollout of Microsoft Visio in the entire office, or a server upgrade. Many people – even project managers and IT directors, seem to compare ITIL Service Management implementation with the implementation of 'off the shelf' software.

This Guide is created to make you – the reader – think about different reasons why implementing ITIL Service Management can NOT be successful with an 'out of the box' approach and mindset. ITIL Service Management only *touches* on technology, and it is not a piece of software.

ITIL Service Management implementation – when performed successfully – will structurally change your organisation, your staff performance, your customer satisfaction and overall delivery capability.

But before we go into that... let's start at the beginning: What exactly is ITIL?

WHAT IS ITIL?

Since its inception in the late 1980's ITIL® has been the framework of choice for many IT organisations across the world. In fact, it has been so popular that ITIL certification is a stated requirement in most Job Advertisements for IT related roles and the framework is taught at Universities as part of their Post-graduate and MBA programs. As a result of industry involvement and the rapidly growing maturity of the IT industry at large, ITIL is now in its 3rd version.

The ITIL V3 framework consists of a library of books that cover the 5 phases of the Service Lifecycle:

Book title	Content – main focus of this phase in the lifecycle
Service Strategy	Discusses the reason WHY the IT service is needed, and to what extent the service would be needed by the customers.
Service Design	Design consideration and Quality criteria for the Service that is to be created AND the environment that is required to support the service to the customer's needs.
Service	Control and risk mitigation strategies while the new – or

Transition	changed – service is moved into the Production environment.
Service Operations	Activities and departments that are needed to support the IT Services on an ongoing basis to the standards that have been agreed upon with the customer.
Continual Service Improvement	Methodologies for the ongoing improvement of the services, the IT environment and its processes.

One important thing to remember is that ITIL is a FRAMEWORK, it is not a prescriptive set of checklists, nor is it a standard. The ITIL books provide the reader with guidelines on what is generally considered to be good practice (based on 20+ years of experience).

The processes described in the books are aimed at the management of activities in an IT organization, irrespective of company size and technology use. The processes are completely independent of any type of hardware or software that is (or will be) available on the market.

In 2005, the International Standards Organisation (ISO) published an independent standard for IT Service Management, called ISO/IEC 20000. This standard consists of BEST

PRACTICE requirements (part I) and guidance (part II) for the control and management of Service Management processes in an IT organisation. This standard is mostly based on the ITIL Framework.

REASONS FOR IMPLEMENTATION

The reason for the implementation of ITIL Service Management is varied, but most of the companies seem to have the desire to formalize their IT Service Management practices to achieve one or more of the following benefits:

- Improve the quality and efficiency of IT Services
- Comply with management or business requirements
- Follow global standards
- Reduce IT Costs
- Achieve regulatory compliance, or standards certification
- Address a specific IT Operational issue

The top benefit gained from ITIL implementation is improved customer satisfaction. Other benefits include delivery of IT services in accordance with agreed service levels and improved IT service reliability.[ii]

When organisations are implementing ITIL Service Management they usually have a team of 1 – 5 internal staff working on the project on a fulltime basis. Approx. 1/3 of organisations also use 1 – 5 external consultants to support with process design and tool implementation.

Factors that contribute to the success of ITIL implementation are:

- Senior Management commitment
- Sufficient Funding
- Effective Change Management
- Existence of an ITSM champion
- Sufficient allocation and provision of ITIL training to IT staff
- Team commitment

HOWEVER, as visualised in figure 1 below, ITIL is only a small component of IT Service Management. The books only cover guidance on the processes, the activities and some of the associated tools and metrics. The other components of IT Service Management are only briefly touched upon in the ITIL core guidance publications. The other components of IT Service Management (technology, people and organisation) are a crucial part in the successful achievement of the desired deliverables and should be planned for.

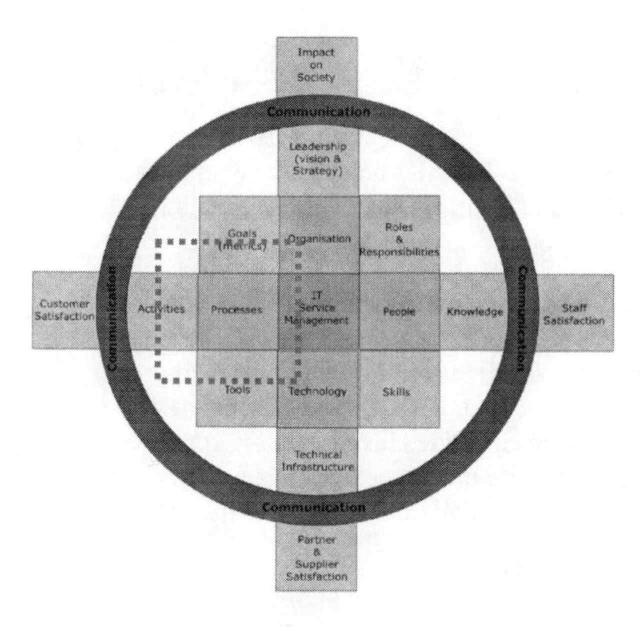
Impact on Society
Communication
Leadership (vision & Strategy)
Goals (metrics)
Organisation
Roles & Responsibilities
Customer Satisfaction
Communication
Activities
Processes
IT Service Management
People
Knowledge
Communication
Staff Satisfaction
Tools
Technology
Skills
Technical Infrastructure
Communication
Partner & Supplier Satisfaction

Figure 1

IMPLEMENTING ITIL

As mentioned in the previous paragraph, ITIL Service Management is a framework. It is not a software application or generic tool. This in itself brings some implementation challenges to the project organisation...

In general, products are easier to implement than frameworks. However, when you begin to implement the ITIL framework, you're suddenly faced with decisions about how to fit your existing process model into the ITIL view. Given that your existing processes are embedded inside existing applications, you will be challenged to wire them together. This will take time and a lot of workshops, discussions and heated debates!

Don't expect to find a single best answer. You must use your training to articulate the tradeoffs of different approaches and the limits of the tools you might employ to automate ITIL-based processes. But perhaps, most importantly, you must move stakeholders to commit to their decisions. Because ITIL doesn't tell people to work in just one way, people may want to hold their options open as long as possible. If you find yourself in this situation, remind your stakeholders that each project is just a step in a long journey. You may revisit a decision in a future phase.

Most companies contemplating an ITIL implementation have developed a methodology to execute projects. Fewer companies have mechanisms for managing groups of related projects over multiple years (and don't forget that your key people might actually change company during the time that you are working on the implementation project). You will have to engage in ongoing awareness campaigns and education programs.

Given that ITIL implementations very often span years and projects typically have shorter durations, you may want to create a team that exists beyond the lifespan of an individual project--a program group. The program group's responsibility is to ensure continuity of vision during the course of the entire implementation and to arbitrate conflicts between projects running parallel.

IMPLEMENTATION OF SERVICE STRATEGY

Strategic positions are converted into plans with goals and objectives for execution through the Service Lifecycle. Figure A outlines the process whereby positions are driven by the need to service specific customers and market spaces and are influenced by strategic perspectives as a service provider.

Plans are the means of achieving those positions. They include the Service Catalogue, Service Pipeline, Contract Portfolio, financial budgets, delivery schedules, and improvement programs. Plans will ensure that each phase in the Service Lifecycle has the capabilities and resources necessary to reach strategic positions. Clarity and context for the development of these is provided by the Service Lifecycle.

The intent of strategy into action through Service Design, Service Transition, Service Operation and Service Improvement is translated through plans. Service Strategy provides input to each phase of the Service Lifecycle and Continual Service Improvement provides the feedback and learning mechanism by which the execution of strategy is controlled.

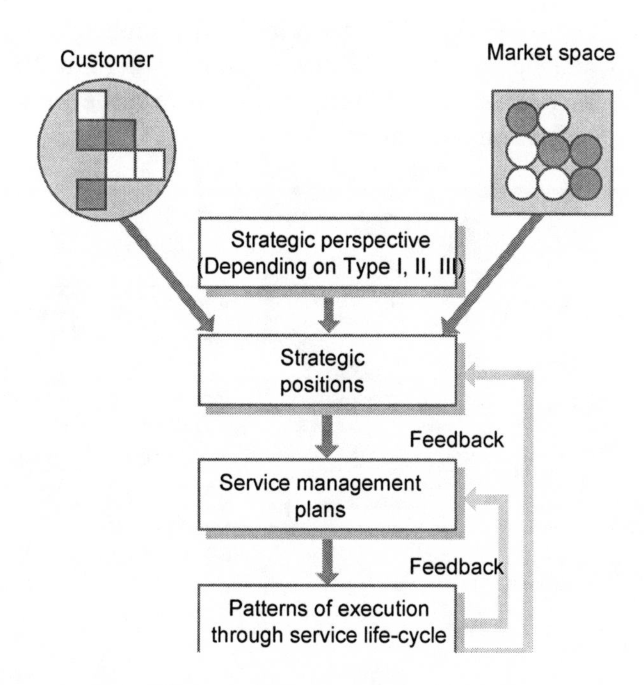

Figure 2

Top Down

Within any given market space, Service Strategy defines the portfolio of services to be offered and the customers to be supported (see Figure 3). This, in turn, determines the Contract Portfolio that needs to be supported with design, transition and operation capabilities. The systems, processes, knowledge, skills and experience required at each phase define the lifecycle capabilities. Interactions between service management capabilities are clearly defined and managed for an integrated and systematic approach to service management. The type of transition capabilities required is determined by Service Desk and Operation capabilities. They also determine the portfolio of service design and the operating range of the service provider in terms of models and capacities.

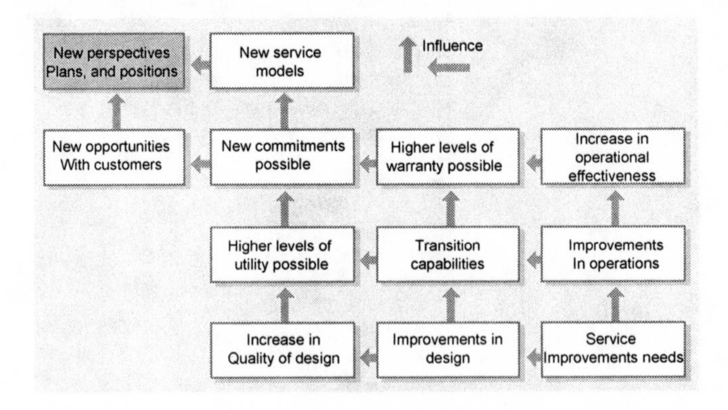

Figure 3

Transition capabilities determine the costs and risks managed by a service provider. The capabilities of the service transition phase determine how quickly a service is transitioned from design to operations. Transition capabilities reduce the costs and risks for customers and service providers throughout the lifecycle by maintaining visibility and control over all service management systems and processes. Not only acting as filters, transition capabilities act as amplifiers that increase the effectiveness of design and operation. Transition capabilities interact with service designs to provide new and improved service models. They also interact with operation models and capacity to increase the operational effectiveness of plans and schedules. The net effect is the service levels delivered to customers in fulfilment of contracts.

Service providers and customers each face strategic risks from uncertainties. It is impossible to either control or predict all the factors in a business environment. The risks may translate into opportunities or challenges depending on the alignment between service management capabilities and the emergent needs of customers. Continual Service Improvement is required for Service Strategy to drive feedback through the Lifecycle elements to ensure that challenges and opportunities are not mismanaged (Figure 4).

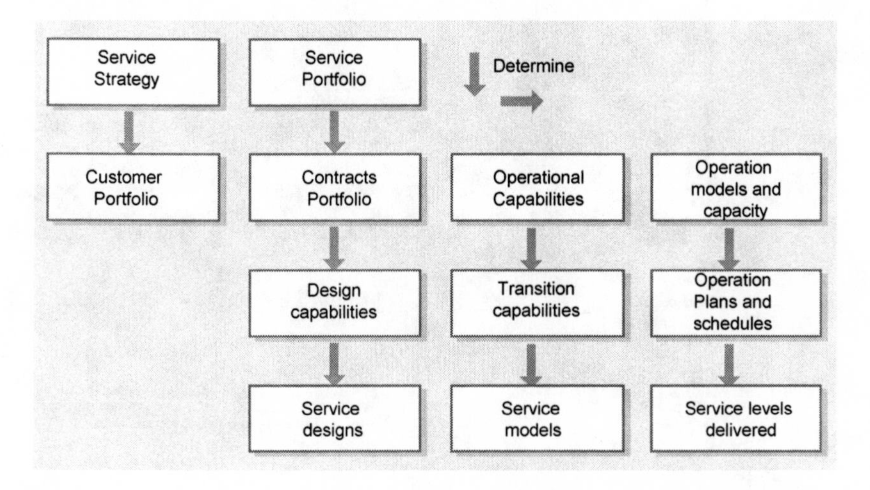

Figure 4

New strategic positions are adopted based on patterns that emerge from executing the Service Lifecycle. In order to form a closed-loop planning and control system for service strategies, bottom-up development of Service Strategy is combined with the traditional top-down approach (Figure 5). Such feedback and learning is critical to the success factor for service management to drive changes and innovation.

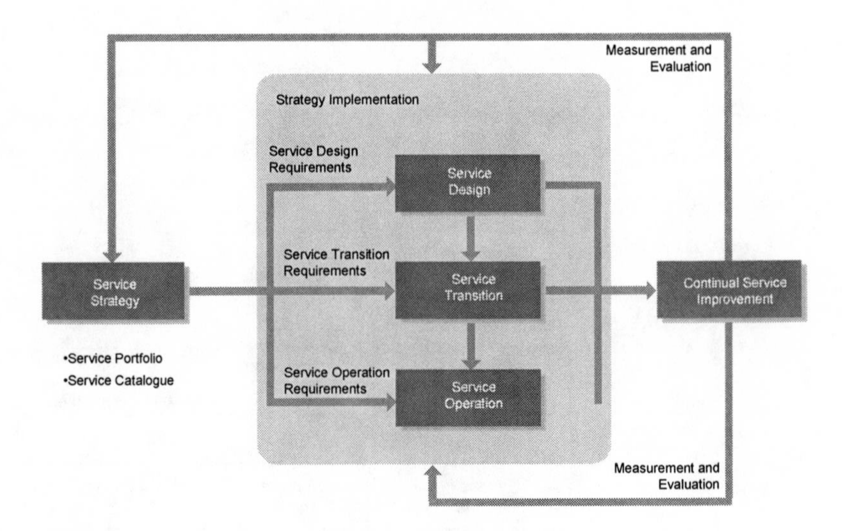

Figure 5

IMPLEMENTING SERVICE DESIGN

This section considers the task of implementing the Service Design processes and covers issues such as:

- Where do we start?
- How do we improve?
- How do we know we are making progress?

The activities of implementing and improving Service Design need to be focused on the needs and requirements of the customer and the business. These activities should be prioritized by:

- Business needs and business impacts
- Risks to the services and processes.

The activities will be dictated by the requirements documented in the Service Level Requirements and the Service Level Agreements.

Business Impact Analysis

The BIA is an ongoing source of valuable input when trying to establish business needs, impacts and risks. It is an essential tool used by the overall Business Continuity process and will dictate the strategy for risk reduction and disaster recovery. The BIA will show which parts of the organization will be effected by a major incident and what effect that will have on the company as a whole. This in turn identifies the most critical business functions on which the company's survival depends. In addition, data from the BIA can provide valuable input in to a number of other areas as well and enables a greater understanding of the service that would have otherwise been available.

The BIA can be divided into two areas:

- *Business Management*; which has to investigate the impact of the loss of a business process or a business function. This would also include the knowledge of manual workarounds and the associated costs.
- *Service Management*; it is essential to break down the effects of service loss to the business. This element of the BIA shows the impact of service disruption to the business. The services can be managed and influenced by Service Management. Other aspects also covered in 'Business BIA' cannot be influenced by Service Management.

As part of the design phase of a new or changed service, a BIA should be conducted to help define the business continuity strategy and to enable a greater understanding about the function and importance of the service. This will enable the organization to define:

- Which are the critical services, what constitutes a major incident on these services, and the subsequent impact and disruption caused to the business – important in deciding when and how to implement changes
- Acceptable levels and times of service outage levels – also important in the consideration of change and implementation schedules
- Critical business and service periods – important periods to avoid
- Cost of loss of service – important for Financial Management
- Potential security implications of a loss of service – important consideration in the management of risk.

Service Level Requirements (SLR's)

SLR's for all services will be identified and the ability to deliver against these requirements assessed and finally agreed in a formal Service Level Agreement. For new services, the requirements must be identified at the beginning of the development process, not after completion. Building a service with the SLR's leading the way is an essential factor from a Service Design perspective.

Risks to the Service and Processes

When implementing the Service Design phase and ITSM processes, business-as-usual practices must not be adversely affected. This aspect must be considered during the production and selection of the preferred solution to ensure that disruption to operational services is minimized. The assessment of risk should then be considered in detail during the Service Transition phase activities as part of the implementation process.

Implementing Service Design

The process, policy and architecture for the design of services outlined in this publication will need to be documented and utilized to ensure the appropriate innovative IT services can be designed and implemented to meet current and future agreed business requirements.

The question often asked is 'which process do I implement first?' The most correct answer is all of them, as the true value of implementing all of the Service Management processes is far greater than the sum of the individual processes. All of the processes are interrelated, and in some cases are totally dependent on others. What is ultimately required is a single, integrated set of processes, providing management control of a set of IT services throughout their entire lifecycle.

However, in reality it is unlikely that organizations can do everything at once. In this situation it is recommended that the areas of greatest need are addressed first. A detailed assessment needs to be undertaken to ascertain the strengths and weaknesses of IT service provision. This should be undertaken by performing customer satisfaction surveys, talking to customers, talking to IT staff and analyzing the processes in action. From this assessment, short to medium and long term strategies can be developed.

It may be that 'quick wins' need to be implemented in the short term to improve the current situation, but these improved processes may have to be discarded or amended as part of the medium to long term strategies. If 'quick wins' are implemented, it is important that they are not done at the expense of the long-term objectives, so these must be considered at all times. However, every organization will have to start somewhere, and the starting point will be wherever the organization is now in terms of IT Service Management maturity.

Implementation priorities should be set against the goals of a Service Improvement Plan (SIP). Throughout the implementation process, key players must be involved in the decision making process. There can be a tendency, when analyzing the areas of greatest need, to go straight for tools to improve the situation. Workshops or focus groups will be beneficial in understanding the requirements and the most suitable process for implementation that will include people, processes, products and partners.

Step one is to establish a formal process, method of implementation and improvement of Service Design, with the appropriate governance in place. This formal process should be based around the six stage process of the Continual Service Improvement cycle.

It is important that when implementing or improving processes a structured Project Management method is used. The improvement process can be summarized as understanding the vision by ascertaining the high-level business objectives. The 'vision-setting' should set and align business and IT strategies and assess the current situation to identify strengths that can be built on weaknesses that need to be addressed.

The following are key elements for successful alignment of IT with business objectives:

- Vision and leadership is setting and maintaining strategic direction, clear goals, and measurement of goal realization in terms of strategic direction
- Acceptance of innovation and new ways of working
- Thorough understanding of the business, its stakeholders and its environment
- IT staff understanding the needs of the business
- The business understanding the potential
- Informational and communication available and accessible to everyone who needs it
- Separately allocated time to familiarize with the material
- Continuous tracking of technologies to identify opportunities for the business.

The implementation/improvement cycle is useful in checking the alignment between the business and IT.

Measurement of Service Design

The success of the Service Design phase and the success of the improvement to the processes around Service Design must be measured; the data must be analyzed and reported on. Where the design or process does not meet the requirements of the business as a whole, changes to the process may be required and the results of the changes must also be measured. Continuous measurement, analysis and reporting are mandatory requirements for both the Service Design process and the ITSM processes.

There are measurement methods available that enable the analysis of service improvement. The Balanced Scorecard is a method developed by Robert Kaplan and David Norton as a concept for measuring company activities in terms of its vision and strategies. It gives a comprehensive view of the performance of the business. The system forces managers to focus on the important performance metrics that drive success. It balances a financial perspective with customers, internal process and learning and growth perspectives.

More information can be found on the Balanced Scorecard at www.scorecardsupport.com

Six Sigma is a methodology developed by Bill Smith at Motorola Inc. in 1986. It was originally designed to manage process variations that cause defects, defined as unacceptable deviation from the mean or target, and to systematically work towards managing variation to eliminate those defects. Six Sigma has now grown beyond defect control and is often used to measure improvement in IT process execution. More information can be found on Six Sigma at http://www.isixsigma.com

Six Sigma (DMADV) is an improvement system used to develop new processes at Six Sigma quality levels and is defined as:

Define – formally define the goals of the design activity that are consistent with customer demands and organization strategy

Measure – identify Critical Success Factors, capabilities, process capability and risk assessment

Analyze – develop and design alternatives, create high level design and evaluate capability to select the best design

Design – develop detailed design, optimize design and plan for design verification

Verify – set up pilot runs, implement production process and hand over to process owners.

This process is an improvement system for existing processes falling below specification and looking for incremental improvement.

Prerequisites for Success

There are several prerequisites needed for the Service Design phase and the successful introduction of new or revised processes. Often these prerequisites for success are elements of one process required by another. For example, fully completed and up-to-date Business Service Catalogue and Technical Service Catalogue are required before Service Level Management can design the SLA and supporting agreement structure, and before SLM can set up and agree the SLA's. Problem Management will depend on a mature Incident Management process.

The prerequisites for success can be much wider than just ITSM process interdependencies. For example, the design of availability and capacity for a new service cannot be achieved without details of the business plan for the utilization of the new service. The design of service will be impossible without the Service Portfolio and Service Transition pack.

There are more examples of these prerequisites for success that need to be considered and planned before high process maturity levels can be achieved. Low maturity in one process will mean that high levels of maturity will not be achievable in other processes.

IMPLEMENTING SERVICE TRANSITION

Implementing Service Transition in an organization when this has not existed before is only likely if a new service provider is being established. Therefore, the task for most service provider organizations will be one of service improvement, a matter of assessing their current approach to the Service Transition processes and establishing the most effective and efficient improvements to make, prioritized according to the business benefit that can be achieved.

Implementing new or improved Service Transition processes will be a significant organizational change and an introduction of improved services delivered by the service provider. From that context, much of the guidance in this publication on delivering new or changed services is directly applicable to introducing Service Transition itself. In doing so, is in itself, a Service Transition exercise, since it is changing the services delivered by the service provider.

Stages of Introducing Service Transition

These stages will match those of other services, requiring a justification for the introduction, designing of the Service Transition components and then their introduction to the organization (transitioning) before they can run in normal mode.

Justifying Service Transition

Service Transition is a key contributor to the service provider's ability to deliver quality services to the business. It is the delivery mechanism between the work of design, and the day-to-day care delivered by operations. However, Service Transition processes are not always visible to customers, and this can make financial justification difficult. When setting up Service Transition, attention needs to be paid to ways of quantifying and measuring the benefits, typically as a balance between impact to the business (negative and positive) and cost (in terms of money/staff resources) and in terms of what would be prevented by applying resources to any specific transition, such as delivering staff resources or delaying implementation.

Gathering of evidence on the cost of current inadequate Service Transition is a valid and useful exercise, addressing issues such as:

- Cost of failed changes
- Extra cost of actual transition compared with budgeted costs
- Errors found in live running that could have been detected during test transition.

Designing Service Transition

Useful factors to consider when designing Service Transition are:

Applicable standards and policies

Consider how agreed policies, standards and legislation will constrain the design of Service Transition. Considerations might include requirements for independence and visible accountability.

Relationships

Other internal support services: there are many situations when Service Transition must work together with other areas that are transitioning other elements of a business change, such as HR, facilities management, production control, education and training. The processes will be designed to facilitate these relationships. The aim should be to ensure that ownership for each component of the overall service package is defined and subsequently management responsibility is clear.

Program and project management

Major transition may be managed as programs or projects, and Service Transition will deliver their role within the appropriate umbrella. To ensure appropriate transition is delivered, staff will be involved in agreeing key program and project milestones and timelines and Service Transition should be set up to adopt this role.

To be effective, Service Transition needs to take a broader view across projects, combining transitions and releases to make the best use of available resources.

Internal development teams and external suppliers

Communication channels will need to deal with defects, risks and issues discovered during the transition process. Channels to both internal teams and external suppliers will need to be identified and maintained.

Customers/user

Communication with customers and users is important to ensure that the transitioned service will remain focused on current business requirements. The requirements at actual transition may evolve from the needs identified at design stage and communication channels with the customer will be the source of identifying those changes. Effective communication will benefit from an agreed strategic stakeholder contact map. In many circumstances this communication will be routed through service or account management or Service Level Management, but these channels need to be identified and designed into the Service Transition processes also.

Other stakeholders

Other stakeholders will need to interface with Service Transition and these should be identified for all foreseeable circumstances, including in disaster recovery scenarios, and so liaison with

ITSCM should be created for. Other possible considerations might include:

- IT e.g. networks, IT security, data management
- Outside of IT but within the organization e.g. facilities management, HR physical security
- Outside of the organization e.g. landlords, police and regulatory bodies.

Budget and resources

Funding approach

A mechanism for controlling the funding of the transition infrastructure needs to be established, this will need to include:

- Testing environments
- SCM and Service Knowledge Management Systems

The costing of transition objectives needs to be an essential inclusion of design. Often the transition options will be costed and a business risk-based decision reached.

Resources

Similar to the issues and options identified in the funding area, supply and control of other resources will need to be addressed within the Service Transition such as:

- Staff

- Central Infrastructure

Test environment management is a major item of expenditure and a significant resource element in many organizations. Under funding/resourcing can cause very expensive errors and problems in supporting live services, and have severe detrimental effects on an organization's overall business capability.

Risk & Value

As with all transitions, decisions around transitioning the transition service should not be made without adequate understanding of the expected risks and benefits. Risks may include:

- Alienation of support staff
- Excessive costs to the business
- Unacceptable delays to business benefits.

The risks and beneficial values require a baseline of the current situation, if the changes are to be measureable. Measures of the added value from Service Transition might include:

- Customer and user satisfaction
- Reduced incident and failure rates for transitioned services
- Reduced cost of transitioning.

IMPLEMENTING SERVICE OPERATION

This section focuses on generic implementation guidance for Service Operation as a whole.

Managing Change in Service Operation

The purpose of Service Operation is to achieve stability. Service Operation staff must ensure that changes are absorbed without adverse impact upon the stability of the IT services.

Change Triggers

There are many things that can trigger a change in the Service Operation environment. They include:

- New or upgraded hardware or network components
- New or upgraded applications software
- New or upgraded system software (operating system, utilities, middleware etc. including patches and bug fixes)
- Legislative, conformance or governance changes
- Obsolescence – some components may become obsolete and require replacement or cease to be supported by the supplier/maintainer

- Business imperative – you have to be flexible to work in ITSM, particularly during Service Operation, and there will be many occasions when the business needs IT changes to meet dynamic business requirements
- Enhancements to processes, procedures and/or underpinning tools to improve IT delivery or reduce financial costs
- Changes of management or personnel (ranging from loss or transfer of individuals right through to major take-over's or acquisitions)
- Change of service levels or in service provision – outsourcing, in-sourcing, partnerships, etc.

Change Assessment

In order to ensure that operational issues are taken into account, Service Operation staff must be involved in the assessment of all changes. This involvement should commence as soon as possible to ensure that they have influence over fundamental decisions. The Change Manager must inform all affected parties of the change being assessed in order for input to be prepared and available prior to Change Advisory Board meetings.

It is important that Service Operation staff are involved in the latter stages of the process, as they may be involved in the implementation and wish to ensure that careful scheduling takes place to avoid potential contentions or particularly sensitive periods.

Measurement of Successful Change

The ultimate measure of the success of changes made to Service Operation is that customers and users do not experience any variation or outage of service. The effects of change should be invisible where possible, aside from any enhanced functionality, quality or financial savings resulting from the change.

Service Operation and Project Management

Service Operation is often viewed as 'business as usual' and focused on executing defined procedures in a standard way. Because of this, there is a tendency not to use Project Management processes when they would be appropriate. For example, major infrastructure upgrades, or the deployment of new or changed procedures, are significant tasks that should utilize formal Project Management to improve control and manage costs/resources.

Using Project Management to manage these types of activity would have the following benefits:

- The project benefits are clearly stated and agreed
- There is more visibility of what is being done and how it is being managed, which makes it easier for other IT groups and the business to quantify the contributions made by operational teams
- This in turn makes it easier to obtain funding for projects that have traditionally been difficult to cost justify
- Greater consistency and improved quality

- Achievement of objectives results in higher credibility for operational groups.

Assessing and Managing Risk in Service Operation

There are a number of occasions where it is imperative that risk assessment to Service Operation is undertaken and acted upon quickly.

Assessing the risk of potential changes or Known Errors is the most obvious area. Service Operation staff may also need to be involved in assessing the risk and impact of:

- Failures, or potential failures – either reported by Event Management or Incident/Problem Management, or warnings raised by manufacturers, suppliers or contractors
- New projects that will ultimately result in delivery into the live environment
- Environmental risk (encompassing IT Service Continuity-type risks to the physical environment and locale as well as political, commercial or industrial-relations related risks)
- Suppliers, particularly where new suppliers are involved or where key service components are under the control of third parties
- Security risks – both theoretical or actual arising from security related incidents or events
- New customers/services to be supported.

Operational Staff in Service Design and Transition

All IT groups will be involved during Service Design and Service Transition to ensure that new components of service are designed, tested and implemented to provide the correct levels of functionality, usability, availability, capacity, etc.

During the early stages of Service Design and Service Transition, Service Operation staff must be involved to ensure that when new services reach the live environment, they are fit for purpose and are 'supportable' in the future.

In this context, 'supportable' means:

- Capable of being supported from a technical and operational viewpoint from within existing, or pre-agreed additional resources and skills levels
- Without adverse impact on other existing technical or operational working practices, processes or schedules
- Without any unexpected operational costs or ongoing or escalating support expenditure
- Without any unexpected contractual or legal complications
- No complex support paths between multiple support departments of third-party organizations.

Note: Change is not just about technology. It also requires training, awareness, cultural change, motivational issues and more.

Planning and Implementing Service Management Technologies

In order to plan for in readiness for, and during deployment and implementation of, ITSM support tools, organizations need to consider the following factors.

Licences

The overall cost of ITSM tools is usually determined by the number and type of user licences required.

Often sold in modular format, the exact functionality of each module needs to be well understood. Initial sizing must be conducted to determine the number and type of users that will need to access each module.

Licences are often available in the following types:

Dedicated Licences

Staff that require frequent and prolonged use of the module will use dedicated licences. For example, Service Desk staff will need a dedicated licence to use an Incident Management module.

Shared Licences

For staff that make fairly regular use of the module, but not on a day-to-day basis, a shared licence will usually suffice. For example, third-line support staff may need regular access to an Incident Management module, but only when an incident record is being updated. It is important to estimate the ratio of required licences depending on the number of potential users, the length of periods of use and the expected frequency between usages.

The cost of a shared licence is usually more expensive than that of a dedicated licence. However, due to the nature of a shared licence, fewer are required and therefore the cost will be less.

Web Licences

Web licences allow some form of 'light interface' via web access to the tool capabilities. They are usually suitable for staff requiring remote access, occasional access or usage of just a small subset of functionality. For example, engineering staff may wish to log details of actions taken on incidents.

The cost of a web licence is usually a lot less than other licences, as the ratio of use is often much lower.

It is important to note that some staff may require access to multiple licences. For example, support staff may require a dedicated or shared licence during the day, but may require a web licence for out of hours support.

Service on Demand

There is a trend within the IT industry for suppliers to offer IT applications 'on demand', where access is given to the application for a period of demand and then severed when it is no longer required. This may be useful either for smaller organizations or if the tools in question are very specialized and used infrequently.

Alternately, the use of a tool can be offered as part of a specific consultancy assignment. For example, a specialist Capacity management consultancy may offer a regular but relatively infrequent Capacity Planning consultancy package and provide use of the tools for the duration of the assignment. Licence fees are likely to be included as part of, or as an addendum to, the consultancy fee.

A further variation is where software is licensed and charged on an agent/activity basis. An example of this is interrogation/monitoring and/or simulation software. For example, agent software that can simulate pre-defined customer paths through an organization's website to assess and report upon performance and availability. This type of software is typically charged based on the number of agents, their location and/or the amount of activity generated.

Full investigations of the licensing structure must be investigated and well understood before the tools are deployed.

Deployment

Before many ITSM tools can be used, particularly Discovery and Event Monitoring tools, they require some client/agent software deploying to all target locations. This needs careful planning and execution, and should be handled through formal Release and Deployment Management.

Careful scheduling and testing is needed even where network deployment is possible. Records must be maintained throughout the rollout so that support staff have knowledge of who has been upgraded and who has not. Interim Change Management may be necessary and the CMS should be updated as the rollout progresses.

The reboot of the devices for the client software to be recognized is often necessary and needs to be arranged in advance. Long delays can occur if staff do not generally switch off their desktops overnights. Further arrangements may also be necessary for staff to log on and receive new software.

Capacity Checks

In order to ensure that all of the target locations have sufficient storage and processing capacity to host and run the new software, Capacity Management may be needed in advance. Those that cannot will need upgrading or renewal and lead times for this must be included in the plans.

The capacity of the network should also be checked to establish whether it can handle the transmission of management information, log files and the distribution of clients and possibly software and configuration files.

Timing of Technology Department

Care is needed in order to ensure that tools are deployed at the appropriate time in relation to the organization's level of ITSM sophistication and knowledge. It may be seen as an immediate panacea if tools are deployed too soon and any necessary action to change processes, working practices or attitudes may be hindered or overlooked.

The organization must first examine the processes that the tool is seeking to address and also ensure that staff are 'brought in' to the new processes and way of working and have adopted a 'service culture'.

However, tools are tangible and can, and often do, make things a reality for many people. Technical staff can immediately see how the new processes can work and the benefits they may provide.

Without adequate tooling, some processes simply cannot be done. There must be a careful balance to ensure that tools are introduced when they are needed and not before.

Care is also needed to ensure that training in any tools is provided at the correct point. If the training is too early, knowledge will be diminished or be lost. However, staff will need to be formally trained and fully familiarized with the operations of the tools well in advance of live deployment. Additional training should be planned as needed once the tools go live.

Type of Introduction

A decision is needed on what type of introduction is needed – whether to go for a 'Big Bang' introduction or some sort of phased approach. A phased approach is more likely to be necessary as most organizations will not start from a 'green field' situation and will have live services to keep running during the introduction.

In most cases, a new tool will be replacing an older, less sophisticated tool. Therefore the changeover between the two must be considered. This often involves deciding what data needs to be carried forward from the old to the new tool and may require significant reformatting to achieve the required results. Ideally this transfer should be done electronically. However, a small amount of re-keying of live data may be inevitable and should be factored into the plans. Older tools generally rely on more manual entry and maintenance of data. For this reason, an audit should be performed to verify data quality when electronic data migration is being used.

Where data transfer is complicated or time consuming to achieve, an alternative might be to allow a period of parallel running. This involves the old tool being available for an initial period alongside the new one. It is advised that the old tool be made 'read-only' in order to ensure that no mistakes can be made logging new data into the old tool.

IMPLEMENTATION OF CSI

Critical consideration for implementing CSI

Before implementing CSI it is important to have identified and filled the critical roles that are required within this phase, such as CSI Manager, Service Owner and Reporting Analyst. A Service Level Manager is also needed to be the liaison between IT and the business.

Where to start?

One approach is to start looking at the handoff of output from the different lifecycle domains. The Service Design phase needs to monitor and report on their activities and by using trend analysis, identify relevant improvement opportunities. This needs to be done during every phase of the service lifecycle, especially during Service Design, Transition and Operation. The Continual Service Improvement phase is engaged in this activity.

Communication strategy and plan

Timely and effective communication forms an important part of any service improvement project. In an effort to transform an organization from performing CSI activities on an ad hoc basis to a more formal and ongoing CSI activities, it is crucial that staff, users and stakeholders are kept up to date of all changes to the processes, activities, roles and responsibilities.

The goal of the communications plan is to build and maintain awareness, understanding, enthusiasm and support among key influential stakeholders for the CSI program. When developing a communication plan, it is important to note that effective communication is not just based on a one-way flow of information, and it is more than just meetings. A communications plan must incorporate the ability to deal with responses and feedback from the targeted audiences.

The plan should include a role to:

- Design and deliver communications to the different CSI roles, stakeholders such as other ITSM process roles and identified target audiences
- Identify forums for customer and user feedback
- Receive and deliver responses and feedback to the project manager and/or process team members.
- Key activities for the communication plan include:
- Identifying stakeholders and target audiences
- Developing communication strategies and tactics
- Identifying communication methods and techniques
- Developing the communications plan
- Identifying the project milestones and related communications requirements.

When developing the communication plan it is important to take into consideration the culture around communication within the business. In some organizations there are strict guidelines on who can communicate with the business. Often times this is through the Service Level Management and Business Relationship Management processes. No matter what the method, communicating with the business should be the key communication activity.

CSI & Organizational Change

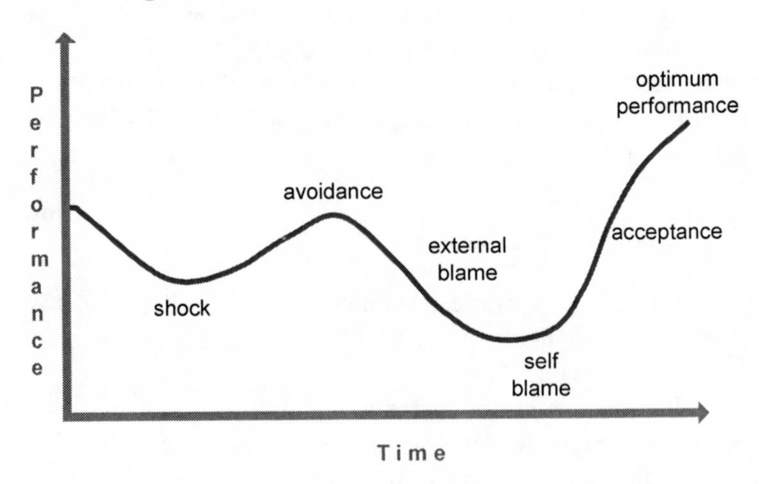

Figure 6

Many organizational change programs fail to achieve the desired results. People generally do not like change, so it is essential that benefits are explained to all parties to obtain and retain support as the change occurs. Communication is key to ensuring a smooth transition from old working practices to new ones. Those responsible for managing and steering the CSI program should consciously address these softer issues. Using an approach such as John P. Kotter's Eight Steps to Transforming your Organization, together with formalized project management skills and practices, will significantly increase the chance of success.

Kotter, Professor of Leadership at Harvard Business School, investigated more than 100 businesses that were involved with or had attempted a complete change program. From this research he identified the 'Eight main reasons why transformation efforts fail' these reasons apply equally to ITSM implementation programs.

1. *Create a sense of urgency*

Half of all transformations fail to realize their goals due to the lack of adequate attention to this step. Not enough people buy into the fact that change is a must. It is essential that all parties understand the repercussions of not making the change as this will help to gain commitment and provide input to a business justification for investing in CSI.

2. *Forming a guiding coalition*

Experience shows a need for assembling a group with sufficient power to lead the change effort and work together as a team. Power means more than simply formal authority but also experience, respect, trust and credibility. This team is the guiding coalition for the CSI phase.

3. *Creating a vision*

This guiding coalition should be responsible for ensuring that a vision is produced describing the aim and purpose of CSI. A good vision statement can service four essential purposes:

- Clarify the direction of the program
- Motivate people to take action in the right direction
- Coordinate the actions of many different people
- Outline the aims of senior management.

4. *Communicating the vision*

Although the vision provides a powerful tool in helping guide and coordinate change, the real power is unleashed when the vision is effectively communicated to the stakeholders. Every stakeholder should understand the vision.

5. *Empowering other to act on the vision*

Establishing urgency, creating a guiding coalition, creating and communicating a vision are all aimed at creating and communicating a vision are all aimed at creating energy, enthusiasm, buy-in and commitment to enable successful change. In the empowering phase, two important aspects need to be stressed: enabling and removing barriers.

6. *Planning for and creating short-term wins*

Implementing service management improvements can be a lengthy program of change. It is important that during the program, short term wins are realized and are communicated. Short-term wins help to keep a change effort on track and help keep the energy and commitment levels high. Real transformation takes time. Without short-term wins, too many people give up or join the ranks of those opposed to change.

7. *Consolidating improvements and producing more change*

The success of short-term wins keeps the momentum going and creates more change. In CSI it is important to recognize short to medium and long term wins. Changes should sink deeply into the new culture or the new approaches will be fragile and subject to regression:

- Short-term wins – have the characteristics of convincing, motivating and showing immediate benefits and gains
- Medium-term wins – have the characteristics of confidence and capability, and having a set of working processes in place.
- Long-term wins – have the characteristics of self learning and expertise, and fully integrated processes that have self-learning and improvement built into them.

8. *Institutionalizing the change*

Change needs to be institutionalized within the organization. Many changes fail because they are not consolidated into everyday practices. Institutionalizing change means showing how new working practices have produced real gain and benefits, and ensuring that the improvements are embedded in all organizational practices.

Often the CSI team is disbanded before the working practices are institutionalized; there is danger that people may revert to old working practices, but this cannot be allowed to happen. CSI must be a way of life, not a reaction to a failure of some description.

CASE STUDIES

1. The German Air Traffic Control

Real life feedback from The German Air Traffic Control[iii] who implemented Service Level Management in 2005 as part of their ITIL Service Management process implementation:

"Today the most critical factor for IT-organization or service provider is the "full-life-support" of

the business processes. The ITIL standard is best practice method for reorganization into a customer

oriented service provider. It is recommend realizing the ITIL processes via organization project. Therefore it is necessary to work out a detail project plan.

The implementation time for the ITIL processes depends on the complexity of IT-organization and on the ITIL process itself. The experience for complex companies shows the following time periods.

- *Incident Management 6-18 months,*
- *Configuration Management 3-9 months,*
- *Problem Management 5-8 months,*
- *Change Management 3-4 months,*
- *Release Management 2-3 months,*
- *Availability Management 4-8 months,*

- *Financial Management 6-12 months,*
- *Service Level Management 6-9 months.*

After the implementation of ITIL it is necessary to define the services and service modules of

the IT-organization; to describe them in detail and to calculate the costs and prices for every service as

well as to provide the service via Service Level Agreement."

2. Telecom company

An international telecom company[iv] with more than 6,500 employees and annual revenue of $4 billion in the US has the following experience:

"Since the ITIL work was done in an ivory tower, the IT staff had not been on board since the project's inception. Communication problems were rampant as both the ITIL team and the IT organization struggled to create a common set of terminology and understand basic ITIL methodologies. Actual workflows and roles proved incompatible with the ideal. Meanwhile, the organization continued to grow, adding new lines of business for VoIP and acquiring another company. Finally, the ITIL initiative was pulled back and assigned to IT architects for overhaul..." The total project took approx. 2 years.

3. State Revenue Office of Victoria

The Sate Revenue office of Victoria (AUS) started an ITIL implementation project[v] when they decided to in-source their IT Services. SRO has approx. 450 staff, and the ITIL implementation project happened between May 2003 and June 2005.

Some of the benefits stated are:

- *Documented IT policies and procedures to an external standard (AS8018)*
- *Greater visibility of changes*
- *Better reporting*
- *Better maintenance of in-sourced environment leading to on-going cost savings and reduced risk*

THE IT SERVICE MANAGEMENT ITIL V3 BENCHMARK CHECKLIST

Here you will find a checklist of ALL activities any IT environment performs or needs to perform in Service Strategy, Design, transition, Operation and improvement.

Many of which touch your role direct – and even more of those can be used by YOU to help grow your organization by pointing out their necessity and benefits. Go through this checklist, check of the ones you and your organization are not doing yet – and prioritize them.

SERVICE STRATEGY - THE PRACTICE OF SERVICE MANAGEMENT

1. Service Management is clearly defined

2. We know what our services are

3. We have decided upon a strategy to serve our customers

4. We know which services we should offer to whom

5. We know how we differentiate ourselves from competing alternatives

6. We know how we truly create value for our customers

7. We know how we capture value for our stakeholders

8. We know how we can make a case for strategic investments

9. Financial management provides visibility and control over value-creation

10. We have defined service quality

11. We know how to choose between different paths for improving service quality

12. We know how to efficiently allocate resources across a portfolio of services

13. We know how to resolve conflicting demands for shared resources

Service Strategy Principles

1. The outcomes that matter are identified and ranked in terms of customer perceptions and preferences

2. We know what our business is

3. We know who our customer is

4. We know what our customer values

5. We know who depends on our services

6. We know how our customers use our services

7. We know why our services are valuable to our customers

8. We know who all the participants in the service are

9. We know the overall patterns of exchange or transactions

10. We know the impacts or deliverables of each transaction on each participant.

11. We know what the best way is to generate value

12. Our strategy captures a more timeless essence of our organization's distinctiveness instead of just the next few years

13. Our strategy is clear and memorable

14. Our strategy has the ability to promote and guide action

15. Our strategy sets boundaries within which people are free to experiment

16. Our positioning guides the organization in making decisions between competing resources and capability investments

17. Our positioning help managers test the appropriateness of a particular course of action

18. Our positioning sets clear boundaries within which staff should and should not operate

19. Our positioning allows freedom to experiment within these constraints

Service Strategy

1. Our service providers have the capabilities to support business activities

2. We know the recurring patterns of activity in the customer's business

3. We know if our customers activity varies based on the time of the year, location, or around specific events

4. There are enough resources to fulfill the demand from the customer's business activity as it occurs

5. We are aware of potential scheduling conflicts that may lead to situations with inadequate capacity

6. We know if the customer's business is subject to regulations

7. Our Service Providers have knowledge and experience with regulatory compliance

8. If services come in direct contact with the customers of customers, we have additional policies and guidelines required to handle user interactions and user information

9. We know who our customers are

10. We know who our customer's customers are

11. We know how we create value for our customers and how they create value

12. We know what assets we deploy to provide value, and which of our clients assets receive value

13. We know which assets we should invest in and which of our assets our clients value most

14. How should we deploy our assets? How do they deploy their assets?

15. We know what services we provide, and what outcomes we support

16. We know what constraints our customers face

17. We know which customer assets we support and what assets we deploy to provide value

18. We know how we deploy our assets

19. We know who the users of our services are

20. We know what type of activity we support and how we create value for them

21. We know how we track performance and what assurances we provide

22. We know our market space

23. We know what our market space wants

24. We are offering unique products/services in our market space

25. Our Market space is not already saturated with good solutions

26. We have the right portfolio of services developed for a given market space

27. We have the right catalogue of services offered to a given customer

28. Every service is designed to support the required outcomes

29. Every service is operated to support the required outcomes

30. We have the right models and structures to be a service provider

31. We know which of our services or service varieties are the most distinctive

32. There are services that the business or customer cannot easily substitute

33. We know which of our services or service varieties are the most profitable

34. We know which customers, channels or purchase occasions are the most profitable

35. We know what makes us special to our business or customers

36. We have measurements that tell us when we are successful and know when that must be achieved.

37. We are not vulnerable to substitution

38. There are means to outperform competing alternatives

39. We know what task or activity the service needs to carry out and what job the customer is seeking to execute

40. We know what outcomes the customer is attempting to obtain and what the desired outcome is

41. We know what constraints may prevent the customer from achieving the desired outcome, and how we can remove these constraints

Service Economics

1. Our differentiation strategy is resulting in higher profits or revenues, lower costs, or greater service adoption

2. The Financial Management process is defined

3. We know which services cost us the most, and why

4. We know our volumes and types of consumed services, and the correlating budget requirement

5. We know how efficient our service provisioning models are relative to alternatives

6. Our strategic approach to service design results in services that can be offered at a competitive market price, substantially reduced risk, or offers superior value

7. We know where our greatest service inefficiencies are

8. We know which functional areas represent the highest priority opportunities for us to focus on as we generate a continual service improvement strategy

9. We know how to select On-shore, Off-shore or Near-Shore services

10. We have defined if we follow Cost Recovery, Value Centre or Accounting Centre principles

11. We know for financial management what deliverable we expect from the implementation

12. We know if the business or IT expects a chargeback system

13. There is currently a Service Catalogue implemented and awaiting pricing

14. We know what our discount rates are

15. Service Portfolio Management is defined

16. We know why a customer should buy our services

17. We know why a customer should buy those services from us

18. We know what the pricing or chargeback models are

19. We know our strengths and weaknesses, priorities and risks

20. We know how our resources and capabilities are to be allocated

21. We know what the long-term goals of the service organization are

22. We know services are required to meet our long term goals

23. We know what capabilities and resources are required for the organization to achieve those services

24. We know how we will get to offer the services that are required to meet our long term goals

Strategy and Organization

1. We have clearly defined where centralized and decentralized management takes place of our services

2. We know if our strategy is based on reducing costs or improving quality

3. We know if our organization has adopted a product or geographic structure

4. We know what obstacles are anticipated for organizational change

5. We have identified the Terminal and instrumental values of the organization

6. We have determined whether the goals, norms and rules of our organization are properly transmitting the value of the organizational culture to staff members and if there are areas for improvement

7. We have assessed the methods we use to introduce new staff and know if these practices help newcomers learn the organizations culture

8. We know if extra value generated from performing an activity inside the organization outweighs the cost of managing it.

9. When deciding to outsource we know if the candidate services improve the business's resources and capabilities

10. When deciding to outsource we know how closely the candidate services are connected to the business's competitive and strategic resources and capabilities

11. When deciding to outsource we know if the candidate services require extensive interactions between the service providers and

the business's competitive and strategic resources and capabilities

12. When deciding to outsource we know if the customer or market space expect us to do this activity

13. The customer or market space will give us credit for performing an outsourcing activity exceptionally well

Strategy to Tactics and Operations

1. We get input from service transition on what the implications are with each strategic choice in terms of costs, time, and risks

2. Regarding our strategic options we know under what scenarios one path is preferable over the other

3. Regarding our strategic options we know what the likelihoods are of those scenarios

4. Regarding our strategic options we know if existing assets can support a transition path

5. Regarding our strategic options we know if there are contingency plans to contain the adverse impact changes

6. Regarding our strategic options we know if a particular change can be implemented fast enough to support the strategy

Technology and Strategy

1. We have service analytics in place to understand how incidents affect services, how the business is impacted and how we respond

2. Our customer encounters are designed considering if customer employees are technical or non-technical

3. We know what the implications are in customer interactions of the technology encounter to the customer

4. With customer encounters we know what the customer expectations and perceptions are

5. We know how we agree on the definition of service levels with respect to a given level of user satisfaction

6. We know how much a customer should agree to pay for a given service level

7. We know what a reasonable timeframe is for a service request to be approved

8. We know what service levels we can impose on an internal function or service group

9. We know how multiple service providers cooperate as an alliance in serving a common customer

10. We know what the delay and the business impact is on the supply chain due to an IT problem

11. We know how long it takes to process procurement orders, and where the worst delays are

12. We know when more than a substantial amount of orders is waiting to go through the distribution systems

13. We know how to ensure good returns from investments made in service assets

14. We know how to find new opportunities for our assets to be deployed in service of new customers

SERVICE DESIGN - SERVICE MANAGEMENT AS A PRACTICE

1. Service Management is clearly defined

2. We know what our services are

3. We are able to measure our processes in a relevant manner

4. The reason our processes exist is to deliver a specific result

5. Every process delivers its primary results to a customer or stakeholder

6. We adopt a holistic approach for all Service Design aspects and areas to ensure consistency and integration

7. We actively manage the design of new or changed services

8. We actively manage the design of the service portfolio, including the Service Catalogue

9. We actively manage the design of the processes required

10. We actively manage the design of measurement methods and metrics

11. We agree service levels, SLAs and targets across the whole enterprise, ensuring critical business processes receive most attention

12. We measure IT quality in business/user terms, reporting what is relevant to users

13. We map business processes to IT infrastructure

14. We map business processes to business and service measurements

15. We map infrastructure resources to services

16. We provide end-to-end online business processes performance monitoring

17. We provide IT Services that are business and customer oriented, focused and driven

18. We provide IT Services that are cost effective and secure

19. We provide IT Services that are flexible and adaptable, yet fit for purpose at the point of delivery

20. We provide IT Services that can absorb an ever-increasing demand in the volume and speed of change

21. We provide IT Services that meet increasing business demands for continuous operation

22. We provide IT Services that are managed and operated to an acceptable level of risk

23. We provide IT Services that are responsive with appropriate availability matched to business needs

24. An IT Strategy or Steering Group carries the overall accountability for setting governance, direction, policy and strategy for IT Services

Service Design Principles

1. New service solutions are added to the service portfolio from the concept phase

2. SLRs for a new service are understood before it goes live

3. Capacity Management is involved in modeling the SLRs

4. Financial Management is involved to set the budget

5. An initial Business impact analysis and Risk assessment is conducted before implementation

6. The Service Desk is made aware of new services, prepared and trained

7. Service transition plans the implementation and builds it into the forward schedule

8. Supplier Management is involved if procurement is required for the new service

9. We design services to satisfy business objectives

10. We design services that can be easily and efficiently developed

11. We design efficient and effective processes

12. We identify and manage risks prior to services becoming live

13. We design secure and resilient IT Services

14. We design measurement methods and metrics for processes and their deliverables

15. We produce and maintain IT design plans

16. We assist in the development of design policies and standards

17. We balance design between functionality, resources and schedules

18. We identify Service Requirements

19. We identify and document Business Requirements and Drivers

20. We collect, analyze and engineer requirements

21. We design appropriate services, technologies, processes that meet business requirements

22. We review and revise all processes and documents involved in service Design

23. We liaison with all other design and planning activities and roles

24. Our service portfolio clarifies why a customer should buy these services

25. Our service portfolio clarifies why customers should buy these services from us

26. Our service Portfolio clarifies what the pricing and chargeback models are

27. We evaluate alternative solutions.

28. We have a procurement process for procuring the preferred solution

29. We use a SOA approach for designing and developing business processes and solutions

30. We use BSM to enable It components to be linked to business goals

Service Design Processes

1. We have defined Service Catalogue Management's Purpose, Goal and Objective

2. We have defined Service Catalogue Management's Scope

3. We have defined Service Catalogue Management's Value to the business

4. We have defined Service Catalogue Management's Policies, Principles and basic concepts

5. We have defined Service Catalogue Management's Process Activities, Methods and Techniques

6. We have defined Service Catalogue Management's Triggers, Inputs, Outputs and interfaces

7. We have defined Service Catalogue Management's KPIs

8. We have defined Service Catalogue Management's Challenges, Critical Success Factors and Risks

9. We have defined Capacity Management's Purpose, Goal and Objective

10. We have defined Capacity Management's Scope

11. We have defined Capacity Management's Value to the business

12. We have defined Capacity Management's Policies, Principles and basic concepts

13. The Business Capacity Management sub-process is defined

14. The Service Capacity Management sub-process is defined

15. The Component Capacity Management sub-process is defined

16. We have defined Capacity Management's Process Activities, Methods and Techniques

17. The underpinning activities (tuning, utilization and response time monitoring etc.) of Capacity Management are defined

18. Threshold management and control is defined

19. Demand Management is defined

20. Modeling and trending are defined

21. Application sizing is defined

22. We have defined Capacity Management's Triggers, Inputs, Outputs and interfaces

23. We have defined Capacity Management's KPIs

24. We have defined Capacity Management's Information Management reporting

25. We have defined Capacity Management's Challenges, Critical Success Factors and Risks

26. We have defined Availability Management's Purpose, Goal and Objective

27. We have defined Availability Management's Scope

28. We have defined Availability Management's Value to the business

29. We have defined Availability Management's Policies, Principles and basic concepts

30. We have defined Availability Management's Process Activities, Methods and Techniques

31. The Reactive activities of Availability Management are Defined

32. The Proactive activities of Availability Management are defined

33. We have defined Availability Management's Triggers, Inputs, Outputs and interfaces

34. We have defined Availability Management's KPIs

35. We have defined Availability Management's Information Management reporting

36. We have defined Availability Management's Challenges, Critical Success Factors and Risks

37. We have defined Service Continuity Management's Purpose, Goal and Objective

38. We have defined Service Continuity Management's Scope

39. We have defined Service Continuity Management's Value to the business

40. We have defined Service Continuity Management's Policies, Principles and basic concepts

41. We have defined Service Continuity Management's Process Activities, Methods and Techniques

42. Service Continuity Management's Stage 1: Initiation is defined

43. Service Continuity Management's Stage 2: Requirements and Strategy is defined

44. Service Continuity Management's Stage 3: Implementation is defined

45. Service Continuity Management's Stage 4:On-going Operation is defined

46. We have defined Service Continuity Management's Triggers, Inputs, Outputs and interfaces

47. We have defined Service Continuity Management's KPIs

48. We have defined Service Continuity Management's Information Management reporting

49. We have defined Service Continuity Management's Challenges, Critical Success Factors and Risks

50. We have defined Information Security Management's Purpose, Goal and Objective

51. We have defined Information Security Management's Scope

52. We have defined Information Security Management's Value to the business

53. We have defined Information Security Management's Policies, Principles and basic concepts

54. We have a defined Security Framework

55. We have an Information Security Policy

56. We have an Information Security Policy Management System

57. We have defined Information Security Management's Process Activities, Methods and Techniques

58. Information Security Management's Security Controls are defined

59. Information Security Management's Management of security breaches and incidents is defined

60. We have defined Information Security Management's Triggers, Inputs, Outputs and interfaces

61. We have defined Information Security Management's KPIs

62. We have defined Information Security Management's Information Management reporting

63. We have defined Information Security Management's Challenges, Critical Success Factors and Risks

64. We have defined Supplier Management's Purpose, Goal and Objective

65. We have defined Supplier Management's Scope

66. We have defined Supplier Management's Value to the business

67. We have defined Supplier Management's Policies, Principles and basic concepts

68. We have defined Supplier Management's Process Activities, Methods and Techniques

69. We have defined how we evaluate new suppliers and contracts

70. We maintain a SDC (supplier and Contracts Database)

71. We have defined how we establish new suppliers and contracts

72. We have defined how we manage supplier, contract management and performance

73. We have defined how we manage contract renewal and / or termination

74. We have defined Supplier Management's Triggers, Inputs, Outputs and interfaces

75. We have defined Supplier Management's KPIs

76. We have defined Supplier Management's Information Management reporting

77. We have defined Supplier Management's Challenges, Critical Success Factors and Risks

Service Design Technology Related Activities

1. Defining Functional requirements is an integral part of requirements engineering

2. Defining Management and operational requirements is an integral part of requirements engineering

3. Defining Usability requirements is an integral part of requirements engineering

4. Interviews are used as a Requirements investigation technique

5. Workshops are used as a Requirements investigation technique

6. Observation is used as a Requirements investigation technique

7. Protocol analysis is used as a Requirements investigation technique

8. Shadowing is used as a Requirements investigation technique

9. Scenario analysis is used as a Requirements investigation technique

10. Prototyping is used as a Requirements investigation technique

11. Requirements are documented in a standardized way in the requirements catalogue

12. Management of Data resources is defined within the scope of Data Management

13. Management of Data/information technology is defined within the scope of Data Management

14. Management of information processes is defined within the scope of Data Management

15. Management of data standards and policies is defined within the scope of Data Management

16. Data is valued as an asset

17. Data is classified as operational, tactical and strategic

18. Data standards are defined and managed

19. Data ownership is defined and managed

20. Data migration is defined and managed

21. Data storage is defined and managed

22. Data capture is defined and managed

23. Data retrieval and usage is defined and managed

24. Data integrity is addressed and managed

25. The application portfolio is described in Application Management

26. Applications and Service Portfolios are linked in Application Management

27. CASE tools and repositories are used and aligned in Application Management

28. The Design of specific applications is managed in Application Management

29. Managing trade-offs is addressed in Application Management

30. The application portfolio is described in Application Management

31. Application Development covers consistent coding conventions

32. Application Development covers application independent building guidelines

33. Application Development covers operability testing

34. Application Development covers management checklists for the building phase

35. Application Development covers organization of the build team roles

36. Major outputs from the development phase are scripts to be run before or after deployment

37. Major outputs from the development phase are scripts to start or stop the application

38. Major outputs from the development phase are scripts to check hardware and software configurations of environments before deployment

39. Major outputs from the development phase are customized scripts to manage the application

40. Major outputs from the development phase are specifications of access control for the system resources used by the application

41. Major outputs from the development phase are specifications of the details required to track an application's major transaction

42. Major outputs from the development phase are SLA targets and requirements

43. Major outputs from the development phase are operational requirements and documentation

44. Major outputs from the development phase are support requirements

45. Major outputs from the development phase are procedures for application recovery and back-ups

13. Our tools enable us to manage the service costs

14. Our tools enable us to manage the relationships, interfaces and inter-dependencies

15. Our tools enable the management of the service portfolio and service catalogue

16. We have a Configuration Management system (CMS)

17. We have a Service Knowledge Management System (SKMS)

Service Design Process Implementation Considerations

1. A Business Impact Analysis is used to define our critical services and what constitutes a Major incident

2. A Business Impact Analysis is used to define acceptable levels and times of service outage levels

3. A Business Impact Analysis is used to define critical business and service periods

4. A Business Impact Analysis is used to define the cost of loss of service

5. A Business Impact Analysis is used to define the potential security implications of a loss of service

6. Service Level Requirements for all services are ascertained

7. Risks to the Services and processes are assessed

8. Service Design is implemented by starting with a Vision, knowing where we are now, where we want to be, how we get there, hoe we will know we have gotten there and how we keep going

9. There are measurement systems in place for Service Design (e.g. Six Sigma)

10. The Prerequisites for success (PFS) are clearly defined

11. The critical success factors and key performance indicators are defined

SERVICE TRANSITION - SERVICE MANAGEMENT AS A PRACTICE

1. Service Management is clearly defined

2. We know what our services are

3. We have clearly defined functions and processes across the lifecycle

4. We are able to measure the processes in a relevant matter

5. The reason a process exists is to deliver a specific result

6. Every process delivers its primary result to a customer or stakeholder

7. The goals of Service Transition are defined

8. The objectives of Service Transition are defined

9. The purpose of Service Transition is Defined

10. The Scope of Service transition is defined

11. Service Transition enables us to align the new or changed service with the customer's business requirements

12. Service Transition ensures that customers and users can use the new or changed service so that it maximizes value to the business

13. We have measurements for alignment with the business and It plans

14. We have measurements for Service Transition

15. Interfaces to other Service Lifecycle stages are clearly defined

Service Transition Principles

1. Service Utilities are Defined

2. Service Warranties are Defined

3. We have defined and implemented a formal policy for service transition

4. We have a policy for implementing all changes to services through service transition

5. We have a policy for adopting a common framework and standards

6. We have a policy for Maximizing re-use of established processes and systems

7. We have a policy for aligning service transition plans with the business needs

8. We have a policy for establishing and maintaining relationships with stakeholders

9. We have a policy for establishing effective controls and discipline

10. We have a policy for providing systems for knowledge transfer and decision support

11. We have a policy for planning release and deployment packages

12. We have a policy for Anticipating and managing course corrections

13. We have a policy for Proactively managing resources across service transitions

14. We have a policy for ensuring early involvement in the service lifecycle

15. We have a policy for assuring the quality of the new or changed service

16. We have a policy for proactively improving quality during service transition

Service Transition Processes

1. The purpose , goal and objective for the Transition Planning and Support process is defined

2. The scope of the Transition Planning and Support process is defined

3. A service transition policy is clearly defined

4. A release policy is clearly defined

5. A transition strategy is clearly defined

6. Service transition preparation activities are defined

7. Service transition is planned and coordinated

8. Advice is given as part of transition process support

9. Administration is organized for transition process support

10. Progress monitoring and reporting is part of process support

11. Triggers, input and Output / Inter-process interfaces are defined

12. Key performance indicators and metrics are defined

13. The purpose, goal and objective for the Change Management process is defined

14. The scope for change management is defined

15. The policies, principles and basic concepts for change management are defined

16. We have defined the types of change requests

17. We have defined standard (pre-authorized) changes

18. Remediation planning for changes is defined

19. Planning and controlling changes is an integrated activity of change management

20. Change and release scheduling is an integrated activity of change management

21. Ensuring there are remediation plans is an integrated activity of change management

22. Measurement and control of changes is an integrated activity of change management

23. Management reporting is an integrated activity of change management

24. Understanding the impact of change is an integrated activity of change management

25. Continual improvement is an integrated activity of change management

26. Raising and recording changes is defined

27. Reviewing the RFC is defined

28. Assessing and evaluating the Change is defined

29. Authorizing the Change is defined

30. Co-coordinating change implementation is defined

31. Reviewing and closing change records is defined

32. Change process models and workflows are defined

33. The Change advisory board is defined

34. Emergency changes are defined

35. Triggers, Input and output and inter-process interfaces are defined

36. Key performance indicators and metrics are defined

37. The purpose, goal and objective for the Service Asset and Configuration Management process is defined

38. The scope for SACM is defined

39. The policies, principles and basic concepts for SACM are defined

40. The Configuration Management System is defined

41. Asset and Configuration Management activities are defined

42. Management and planning for SACM is defined

43. Configuration identification is defined

44. Configuration control is defined

45. Status reporting is defined

46. Verification and audit is defined

47. Triggers, Input and output and inter-process interfaces are defined

48. Key performance indicators and metrics are defined

49. The purpose, goal and objective of the Release and Deployment Management process is defined

50. The scope for Release and deployment is defined

51. The policies, principles and basic concepts for Release and Deployment are defined

52. Release Unit and Identification is defined

53. Release design options are considered

54. Release and deployment models are defined

55. The planning of releases is managed

56. Preparation for build, test and deployment is managed

57. Build and test is managed

58. Service testing and pilots are managed

59. Planning and preparing for deployment are managed

60. Transfer, Deployment and retirement are managed

61. Deployment verification is managed

62. Early life support is managed

63. Review and closing of a deployment is managed

64. Review and closing of the service transition is managed

65. Triggers, Input and output and inter-process interfaces are defined

66. Key performance indicators and metrics are defined

67. The purpose, goal and objective of the Service Validation and Testing process is defined

68. The scope for Service Validation and Testing is defined

69. The policies, principles and basic concepts for Service Validation and testing are defined

70. Inputs from Service Design are defined

71. Service quality and assurance is defined

72. Service Quality, Risk, service transition, release and change management Policies are defined

73. The Test strategy is defined

74. Test Models are defined

75. Validation and testing perspectives are defined

76. Testing approaches and techniques are examined and defined

77. Design considerations are defined

78. Different types of testing are defined

79. Triggers, Input and output and inter-process interfaces are defined

80. Key performance indicators and metrics are defined

81. The purpose, goal and objective of the Evaluation process is defined

82. The scope for Evaluation is defined

83. The policies, principles and basic concepts for Evaluation are defined

84. Service Evaluation terms are defined

85. The Evaluation process is defined

86. The Evaluation plan is defined

87. Evaluation of predicted performance is managed

88. Evaluation of actual performance is managed

89. Risk management is defined

90. Evaluation reporting is defined

91. Triggers, Input and output and inter-process interfaces are defined

92. Key performance indicators and metrics are defined

93. The purpose, goal and objective of the Knowledge Management process is defined

94. The scope for knowledge management Evaluation is defined

95. The policies, principles and basic concepts for Knowledge Management are defined

96. Knowledge management is defined using a DIKW (data - information-knowledge-wisdom) approach

97. A Service Knowledge Management System (SKMA) Is in place to capture and manage knowledge

98. The Knowledge Management Strategy is defined

99. Knowledge Transfer is defined

100. Data and information Management is integrated with Knowledge Management

101. Access and use of the Knowledge Management system is defined

102. Triggers, Input and output and inter-process interfaces are defined

103. Key performance indicators and metrics are defined

Service Transition common operation activities

1. Managing Communication and commitment is a common operation activity

2. Communications during Service Transition are defined

3. Communication planning is managed

4. Different methods of communication are applied

5. Managing Organization and stakeholder Change is a common operation activity

6. The emotional cycle of change is managed

7. Service Transition's role in organizational change is clearly defined

8. Organizational change is planned and implemented

9. A variety of organizational change products is used

10. Organizational readiness for Change is assessed

11. Progress of organizational change is monitored

12. Organization and people issues are dealt with in sourcing changes

13. Organizational Change management's best practices (e.g. Kotter) are applied

14. Stakeholder management is a common operation activity

15. We have a stakeholder management strategy

16. We produce stakeholder maps and analysis

17. Changes in stakeholder commitment are captured

Organizing Service Transition

1. The Process Owner role and the Service Owner role are defined

2. The organizational context for transitioning a service is set

3. Organizational models to support service transition are defined

4. The Service Transition Manager role is defined

5. Planning and support is organized

6. The Service Asset Manager role is defined

7. The Configuration Manager role is defined

8. The Configuration Analyst role is defined

9. The Configuration administrator / librarian role is defined

10. The CMS / Tool administrator role is defined

11. The configuration control board role is defined

12. Change Authority is defined

13. The Change Manager role is defined

14. The Change Advisory Board role is defined

15. Performance and risk evaluation management is defined

16. Service Knowledge management is defined

17. The service test manager role is defined

18. The release and deployment roles are defined

19. The Release packaging and Build roles are defined

20. Deployment is defined

21. Early life support is defined

22. Build and test environment management is defined

23. The Service Transition relationship with other lifecycle stages are defined

Service Transition Technology Considerations

1. A service Knowledge Management system is in place

2. Collaborative, content management, workflow tools are in place

3. Data mining tools are in place

4. Extract, load and transform tools are in place

5. Measurement and reporting system tools are in place

6. Test management and testing tools are in place

7. Database and test data management tools are in place

8. Copying and publishing tools are in place

9. Release and deployment technology tools are in place

10. Deployment and logistics systems and tools are in place

11. Configuration Management systems and tools are in place

12. Version control tools are in place

13. Document-management systems are in place

14. Requirements analysis and design tools, systems architecture and CASE tools are in place

15. Database management audit tools to track physical databases are in place

16. Distribution and installation tools are in place

17. Comparison tools (software files, directories, databases) are in place

18. Build and Release tools (that provide listings of input and output CIs) are in place

19. Installation and de-installation tools (that provide listings of CIs installed) are in place

20. Compression tools (to save storage space) are in place

21. Listing and configuration baseline tools (e.g. Full directory listings with date–time stamps and check sums) are in place

22. Discovery and audit tools (also called 'inventory' tools) are in place

23. Detection and recovery tools (where the build is returned to a known state) are in place

24. Visualization, mapping and graphical representations with drill down reporting tools are in place

Implementing Service Transition

1. Justification of Service Transition is undertaken
2. Designing Service Transition has been done
3. Applicable standards and policies have been researched
4. Relationships have been defined
5. Budgets and resources have been allocated
6. Service transition has been introduced
7. the Cultural change aspects have been addressed
8. Risks and value have been weighed

SERVICE OPERATION - SERVICE MANAGEMENT AS A PRACTICE

1. Service Management is clearly defined

2. We know what our services are

3. We have clearly defined functions and processes across the lifecycle

4. We are able to measure the processes in a relevant matter

5. The reason a process exists is to deliver a specific result

6. Every process delivers its primary result to a customer or stakeholder

7. The goals of Service Operation are defined

8. The objectives of Service Operation are defined

9. The purpose of Service Operation is Defined

10. The Scope of Service Operation is defined

11. The Event Management process is defined

12. The Incident and Problem Management process is defined

13. The Request fulfillment process is defined

14. The Access Management process is defined

15. The Service Desk function is defined

16. The Technical Management function is defined

17. The IT operations Management function is defined

18. The Application Management function is defined

19. Interfaces to other Service Lifecycle stages are clearly defined

Service Operation Principles

1. Distinctive functions, groups, teams, departments and divisions are defined

2. We have a balance between an internal IT view and external business view

3. We balance stability interests versus responsiveness to changes

4. We balance quality of service versus cost of service

5. We balance reactiveness versus proactiveness

6. All Service operation staff is fully aware that they are providing a service to the business

7. We have a clear definition of It service objectives and performance criteria

8. We have linkage of IT Service specifications to the performance of the IT infrastructure

9. We have a definition of operational performance requirements

10. We have a mapping of services and technology

11. We have the ability to model the effect of changes in technology and changes to business requirements

12. We have appropriate cost models to evaluate ROI and cost reduction strategies

13. Operational health is monitored with a set of Vital signs

14. We have routine Operational communication

15. We have formalized communication between shifts

16. We have formalized performance reporting

17. We have formalized communication in projects

18. We have formalized communication related to exceptions

19. We have formalized communication related to emergencies

20. We have training on new or customized processes and service designs

21. We have communication of strategy and design to our service operation teams formalized

22. The means of communication (email, sms etc) are defined

23. We have a structured, regular Operations Meeting

24. We have structured, regular Department, Group and Team Meetings

25. We have structured, regular Customer Meetings

26. We participate in the definition and maintenance of process manuals for all processes we are involved in

27. We establish our own technical procedures manuals

28. We participate in the creation and maintenance of planning documents

29. We participate in the definition and maintenance of Service Management Tool work instructions

Service Operation Processes

1. We have defined Event Management's Purpose, Goal and Objective

2. We have defined Event Management's Scope

3. We have defined Event Management's Value to the business

4. We have defined Event Management's Policies, Principles and basic concepts

5. The "Event Occurs" process activity is specified

6. The "Event Notification" process activity is specified

7. The "Event Detection" process activity is specified

8. The "Event Filtering" process activity is specified

9. The "Significance of Events Categorization" process activity is specified

10. The "Event Correlation" process activity is specified

11. The "Trigger" process activity is specified

12. The "Response Selection" process activity is specified

13. The "Review Actions" process activity is specified

14. The "Close Actions" process activity is specified

15. We have defined Event Management's Triggers, Inputs, Outputs and interfaces

16. We have defined Event Management's KPIs and metrics

17. We have defined Event Management's Information Management reporting

18. We have defined Event Management's Challenges, Critical Success Factors and Risks

19. We have defined Incident Management's Purpose, Goal and Objective

20. We have defined Incident Management's Scope

21. We have defined Incident Management's Value to the business

22. We have defined Incident Management's Policies, Principles and basic concepts

23. Timescales are agreed for all incident handling stages

24. Incident Models are defined

25. Major Incidents are defined

26. The "Incident Identification" process activity is specified

27. The "Incident logging" process activity is specified

28. The "Incident categorization" process activity is specified

29. The "Incident Prioritization" process activity is specified

30. The "Initial Diagnosis" process activity is specified

31. The "Incident Escalation" process activity is specified

32. The "Incident Identification" process activity is specified

33. The "Investigation and Diagnosis" process activity is specified

34. The "Resolution and recovery" process activity is specified

35. The "Incident Closure" process activity is specified

36. We have defined Incident Management's Triggers, Inputs, Outputs and interfaces

37. We have defined Incident Management's KPIs and metrics

38. We have defined Incident Management's Information Management reporting

39. We have defined Incident Management's Challenges, Critical Success Factors and Risks

40. We have defined Request Fulfillment's Purpose, Goal and Objective

41. We have defined Request Fulfillment's Scope

42. We have defined Request Fulfillment's Value to the business

43. We have defined Request Fulfillment's Policies, Principles and basic concepts

44. The "Menu Selection" activity is specified

45. The "Financial approval" activity is specified

46. The "Other approval" activity is specified

47. The "Fulfillment" activity is specified

48. The "Closure" activity is specified

49. We have defined Request Fulfillment's Triggers, Inputs, Outputs and interfaces

50. We have defined Request Fulfillment's KPIs and metrics

51. We have defined Request Fulfillment's Information Management reporting

52. We have defined Request Fulfillment's Challenges, Critical Success Factors and Risks

53. We have defined Problem Management's Purpose, Goal and Objective

54. We have defined Problem Management's Scope

55. We have defined Problem Management's Value to the business

56. We have defined Problem Management's Policies, Principles and basic concepts

57. The "Problem Detection" process activity is specified

58. The "Problem Logging" process activity is specified

59. The "Problem Categorization" process activity is specified

60. The "Problem Prioritization" process activity is specified

61. The "Problem Investigation and Diagnosis" process activity is specified

62. The "Workarounds" process activity is specified

63. The "Raising a known error record" process activity is specified

64. The "Problem Resolution" process activity is specified

65. The "Problem Closure" process activity is specified

66. The "Major Problem Review" process activity is specified

67. The "Errors detected in the development environment" process activity is specified

68. We have defined Problem Management's Triggers, Inputs, Outputs and interfaces

69. The CMS acts as a valuable source for Problem Management

70. We have a Known Error Database to allow quicker diagnosis and resolution

71. We have defined Problem Management's KPIs and metrics

72. We have defined Problem Management's Information Management reporting

73. We have defined Problem Management's Challenges, Critical Success Factors and Risks

74. We have defined Access Management's Purpose, Goal and Objective

75. We have defined Access Management's Scope

76. We have defined Access Management's Value to the business

77. We have defined Access Management's Policies, Principles and basic concepts

78. The "Requesting Access" process activity is specified

79. The "Verification" process activity is specified

80. The "Providing Rights" process activity is specified

81. The "Monitoring Identity Status" process activity is specified

82. The "Logging and Tracking Access" process activity is specified

83. The "Removing or restricting rights" process activity is specified

84. We have defined Access Management's Triggers, Inputs, Outputs and interfaces

85. We have defined Access Management's KPIs and metrics

86. We have defined Access Management's Information Management reporting

87. We have defined Access Management's Challenges, Critical Success Factors and Risks

Common Service Operation Activities

88. We know where we are on the technology centric Vs business centric scale

89. Monitoring and control is a continual cycle

90. We use tools to monitor the status of key CIs and key operational activities

91. We ensure that specified conditions are met (or not met), and if not to raise an alert to the appropriate group (e.g. the availability of key network devices)

92. We ensure that the performance or utilization of a component or system is within a specified range (e.g. disk space or memory utilization)

93. We detect abnormal types or levels of activity in the infrastructure (e.g. potential security threats)

94. We detect unauthorized changes (e.g. introduction of software)

95. We ensure compliance with the organization's policies (e.g. inappropriate use of email)

96. We track outputs to the business and ensure that they meet quality and performance requirements

97. We track any information that is used to measure Key Performance Indicators

98. We use tools to collate the output of monitoring into information that can be disseminated to various groups, functions or processes

99. We interpret the meaning of that information

100. We determining where that information would best be used

101. We ensure that decision makers have access to the information that will enable them to make decisions

102. We route the reported information to the appropriate person, group or tool

103. We use tools to define what conditions represent normal operations or abnormal operations

104. We regulate performance of devices, systems or services

105. We Measure availability

106. We Initiate corrective action, which could be automated (e.g. reboot a device remotely or run a script), or manual (e.g. notify operations staff of the status)

107. We manage the monitor control loop

108. We have defined what needs to be monitored

109. We have internal and external monitoring and control

110. We manage different types of monitoring

111. We monitor in test environments

112. We manage reporting and action upon monitoring

113. We perform service operation audits

114. In IT operations we have a defined Console Management/Operations Bridge

115. In IT operations we have a defined job scheduling role

116. In IT operations we have a defined back-Up and Restore role

117. In IT operations we have a defined Print and Output Role

118. Mainframe management is a mature practice

119. Server Management and support is a mature practice

120. Network management is a mature practice

121. Storage and archive is a mature practice

122. Database Administration is a mature practice

123. Directory Services Management is a mature practice

124. Desktop Support is a mature practice

125. Middleware management is a mature practice

126. Internet/Web Management Mainframe management is a mature practice

127. Facilities and Data Center Management is a mature practice

128. Information Security Management within Service Operation is a mature practice

129. Mainframe management is a mature practice

Organizing Service Operation

1. The Service Desk function is defined

2. We have Justification for and the Role of the Service Desk defined

3. We have Service Desk Objectives

4. We have a clear Service Desk Organizational Structure

5. Service Desk Staffing is managed

6. We have Service Desk Metrics

7. We investigate(d) Outsourcing the Service Desk

8. The Technical Management Role is defined

9. We have clear Technical Management Objectives

10. We have defined Generic Technical Management Activities

11. We have a clear Technical Management Organization

12. We have Technical Design and Technical Maintenance and Support

13. We have Technical Management Metrics

14. We have Technical Management Documentation

15. The IT Operations Management role is defined

16. IT Operations Management Objectives are defined

17. We have a IT Operations Management Organization

18. We have IT Operations Management Metrics

19. We have IT Operations Management Documentation

20. The Application Management Role is defined

21. We have Application Management Objectives

22. We have Application Management Principles

23. The Application Management Lifecycle is defined

24. We have defined Application Management Generic Activities

25. We have a clear Application Management Organization

26. We have defined Application Management Roles and Responsibilities

27. We have Application Management Metrics

28. We have Application Management Documentation

29. We have clear Service Desk Roles

30. We have Technical Management Roles

31. We have IT Operations Management Roles

32. We have Applications Management Roles

33. We have Event Management Roles

34. We have Incident Management Roles

35. We have Request Fulfillment Roles

36. We have Problem Management Roles

37. We have Access Management Roles defined

38. We are organized by Technical Specialization

39. We are organized by Activity

40. We are organized to Manage Processes

41. IT Operations are organized by Geography

42. We have Hybrid Organization Structures of the above

Service Operation Technology Considerations

1. We have Integrated IT Service Management Technology

2. We offer Self Help

3. We have a Workflow or Process Engine

4. We have an Integrated CMS

5. We have Discovery/Deployment /Licensing Technology

6. We have Remote Control

7. We have Diagnostic Utilities

8. We have Reporting facilities

9. We have Dashboards

10. We have Integration with Business Service Management

11. We have Event Management technology

12. We have Incident Management technology

13. We have Integrated ITSM technology

14. We have Workflow and Automated Escalation

15. We have Request Fulfillment applications

16. We have Problem Management applications

17. We have Integrated Service Management Technology

18. We have Change Management applications

19. We have an Integrated CMS

20. We have a Known Error Database

21. We have Access Management applications

22. We have a Service Desk tool

23. We have Service desk specific Telephony infrastructure

24. The Service desk has access to Support Tools

25. We have IT Service Continuity Planning for ITSM Support Tools

Implementing Service Operation

1. We actively Manage Change in Service Operation

2. We monitor and manage Change Triggers

3. We manage Change Assessment

4. We have Measurement of Successful Change defined

5. We Assess and Manage Risks in Service Operation

6. Operational Staff is involved in Service Design and Transition

7. With Planning & Implementing Service Management Technologies we check Licenses

8. With Planning & Implementing Service Management Technologies we check deployment

9. With Planning & Implementing Service Management Technologies we do capacity checks

10. With Planning & Implementing Service Management Technologies we manage the timing of technology deployment

CONTINUAL SERVICE IMPROVEMENT-SERVICE MANAGEMENT AS A PRACTICE

1. Service Management is clearly defined

2. We know what our services are

3. We have clearly defined functions and processes across the lifecycle

4. We are able to measure the processes in a relevant matter

5. The reason a process exists is to deliver a specific result

6. Every process delivers its primary result to a customer or stakeholder

7. The goals of CSI are defined

8. The objectives of CSI are defined

9. The purpose of CSI is Defined

10. The Scope of CSI is defined

11. We have a CSI Plan

12. Our Service improvement, benefits, ROI and VOI outcomes are clearly defined

13. We have CSI justifications for Business drivers and Technology Drivers

14. The business/customer benefits of CSI are clearly defined

15. The financial benefits of CSI are clearly defined

16. The innovation benefits of CSI are clearly defined

17. The IT Organization Internal benefits of CSI are clearly defined

18. The business/customer benefits of CSI are clearly defined

19. Interfaces to other Service Lifecycle stages are clearly defined

CSI Principles

1. CSI is imbedded in organizational change

2. CSI ownership is clearly defined

3. We have role definitions assigned in key activities to key roles

4. We monitor external (regulation, legislation etc.) and internal (org. structure, culture etc.) drivers to CSI

5. We have fully accepted that the IT organization must become a service provider to the business or cease to be relevant

6. We involve the business and determine their service level requirements

7. We define the internal portfolio of Services: services that are planned, in development, in production.

8. We have defined a customer-facing Service Catalogue which details every service and service package offered

9. We Identified internal IT departmental relationships, and codified them with Operational Level Agreements (OLAs)

10. We have identified existing contractual relationships (UCs) with external vendors.

11. We utilize the Service Catalogue as the baseline, negotiate Service Level Agreements (SLAs) with the business

12. We have created a Service Improvement Plan (SIP) to continually monitor and improve the levels of service

13. We have service measurement baselines defined

14. We apply the 7-step improvement process

15. We benchmark our services

16. CSI is aligned with governance programs

17. CSI is aligned with supporting frameworks, models, standards and quality systems

CSI Processes

1. We have defined what we should measure using The 7 Step Improvement Process

2. We have defined what we can measure using The 7 Step Improvement Process

3. We have defined data gathering (who/how/when/integrity of data) using The 7 Step Improvement Process

4. We have defined how we process the data using The 7 Step Improvement Process

5. We have defined how we analyze the data using The 7 Step Improvement Process

6. We have defined how we present and use the information using The 7 Step Improvement Process

7. We have implemented corrective action using The 7 Step Improvement Process

8. We have defined integration with the rest of the lifecycle domains and service management processes

9. We have Technology metrics in place

10. We have Process metrics in place

11. We have Service Metrics in place

12. CSFs and KPIs are defined

13. The purpose, goal and objective for the Service Reporting process is defined

14. We have defined our reporting policy and rules

15. We have defined our service measurement objectives

16. We have defined our CSI policies

17. Monitoring requirements are defined and implemented

18. Data is gathered and analyzed on a consistent basis.

19. Trend reporting is provided on a consistent basis

20. Service Level Achievement reports are provided on a consistent basis

21. Internal and External Service reviews are completed on a consistent basis

22. Services have either clearly defined service levels or service targets

23. Service Management processes have Critical Success Factors and Key Performance Indicators

24. We have defined the Return on Investment (ROI) process for CSI

25. The business case for ROI is established

26. We know what the benefits are of ITIL service improvements

27. We know how it impacts our business

28. We know how revenue is increased with ROI

29. We know our value on investments

30. We know what our ROI is

31. We know what our payback time is

32. We know how ITIL benefits translate to business benefits

33. We measure benefits achieved

34. The business questions for CSI are defined

35. We know where we are now

36. We know what we want

37. We know what we actually need

38. We know what we can afford

39. We know what we will get

40. We know what we did get

41. Service level Management plays a key role in working with the business

42. The goal for the Service Level Management process is defined

43. The service improvement programme is defined

CSI methods and techniques

1. We have defined methods and techniques for CSI

2. We know the efforts and costs for CSI

3. We have a CSI implementation review and evaluation

4. We have CSI assessments

5. We have defined when to assess

6. We have defined what to assess and how

7. We perform Gap analyses

8. We have a benchmarking procedure

9. We know our benchmarking costs

10. We know the value of benchmarking

11. We have defined the benefits of benchmarking

12. We know who is involved in benchmarking

13. We have defined what to benchmark

14. We know what to compare with industry norms

15. Our benchmark approach is well defined

16. We use the balanced score card approach for measuring and reporting

17. We use SWOT analysis

18. We use the Deming Cycle

19. Component Failure Impact analysis (CFIA) is used

20. Fault Tree Analysis (FTA) is used

21. Service Failure Analysis (SFA) is used

22. Technical Observation (TO) is used

23. Business Capacity Management (BCM) is used

24. Service Capacity Management is used

25. Component Capacity Management is used

26. Workload management and demand management are used

27. The iterative activities of Capacity Management are used

28. Business Continuity Management and ITSCM are integrated

29. Risk Management is integrated

30. Problem Management's Post implementation review delivers input to CSI

31. All CSI activities fall under the scope of Change, Release and Deployment Management

32. Inputs on CSIs "What do We Need" are delivered by the Service Knowledge Management system

Organizing for CSI

1. Roles and responsibilities for CSI are defined

2. The CSI activities and skills required are defined

3. We have defined what we should measure

4. We have defined what we can measure

5. We have defined which data is gathered how

6. We have defined how we process the data

7. We have defined how we analyze the data

8. We have defined how we present and use the information

9. We have defined how we implement corrective action

10. The service manager role is defined

11. The CSI manager role is defined

12. The Service owner role is defined

13. The process owner role is defined

14. The Service knowledge management role is defined

15. The reporting analyst role is defined

16. The authority matrix is defined

CSI Technology Considerations

1. We use an IT Service management suite to support CSI activities

2. We use systems and network management tools to support CSI activities

3. We use event management tools to support CSI activities

4. We use automated incident / problem management tools to support CSI activities

5. We use knowledge management tools to support CSI activities

6. We use tools to support CSI activities

7. We use service catalogue and workflow tools to support CSI activities

8. We use performance management tools to support CSI activities

9. We use application and service performance monitoring tools to support CSI activities

10. We use statistical analysis tools to support CSI activities

11. We use software version control tools to support CSI activities

12. We use software test management tools to support CSI activities

13. We use security management tools to support CSI activities

14. We use project and portfolio management tools to support CSI activities

15. We use financial management tools to support CSI activities

16. We use business intelligence and reporting tools to support CSI activities

Implementing CSI

1. The critical roles for CSI have been identified and filled (CSI manager/service owner/reporting analyst)

2. Monitoring and reporting on technology, process and service metrics are in place

3. Internal service review meetings are scheduled

4. Either the service approach or the lifecycle approach is chosen as a basis for CSI implementation

5. Governance is addressed from a strategic view

6. The IT service Management program initiative is defined

7. The business drivers are defined

8. The process changes are defined

9. CSI and organizational change is underpinned by Kotter's change management best practices

10. We have a communication strategy and plan

CONCLUSION

There is a lot more to implementing ITIL Service Management than meets the eye. The ITIL Framework is quite large and at first may be daunting to the IT Director or CIO who is investigating the implementation of the framework in the IT organisation.

The first step is to understand the current situation. Where are we now? What is our current state of affairs? What can stay, and what has to change?

This is also the time when your team will create the vision for the future: where do we want to be? What type of IT organisation do we want to be, and what level of maturity is required? The planning stage of an ITIL Implementation project can last anywhere between a month and a year. However, without this solid planning phase the outcome of the project will most likely be at risk.

Based on the outcome of this assessment a long term plan can be painted as well as a selection of the first few processes that will be improved and implemented.

The design and documentation of the new processes is a (relatively) easy task. The biggest challenge is to create processes that support the overall business vision of the IT shop, and have the full backup and support from the IT staff on the floor.

Because ultimately they need to work with the new and improved processes. Creating a new series of process documents that nobody will read is a waste of money, time and effort. The challenge is to create a series of processes that are adopted by all IT staff in the shop and actively used for the delivery of IT Services to the customers.

The benefits are achievable, and very tangible for most organisations. But only when you realise that implementing this framework is a lot more involved than a simple technology implementation. We are dealing with management processes and the adoption of improved processes by people... and that takes time.

INDEX*

A

B

---

[i] ITIL® is a Registered Trade Mark of the Office of Government Commerce in the United Kingdom and other countries

[ii] Survey conducted by itSMF chapters in Asia in 2008.

[iii] For full case study see: http://www.tsi.lv/Transport&Telecommunication/V65_en/art01.pdf

[iv] For full case study see: http://www.networkworld.com/newsletters/nsm/2006/0306nsm1.html?brl

[v] For full presentation see: http://www.taxadmin.org/fta/meet/06tech/06tech_pres/Broderick.pdf

LaVergne, TN USA
18 March 2010
176394LV00003B/219/P